Explore the Coral Reef

FIRST EDITION
Series Editor Deborah Lock; **US Senior Editor** Shannon Beatty; **Editor** Arpita Nath;
Design Assistant Sadie Thomas; **Art Editor** Dheeraj Arora; **Senior Art Editor** Tory Gordon-Harris;
Producer Sara Hu; **Pre-Production Producer** Nadine King; **Jacket Designer** Natalie Godwin;
Managing Editor Soma Chowdhury; **Managing Art Editor** Ahlawat Gunjan;
Art Directors Rachel Foster and Martin Wilson; **Reading Consultant** Linda Gambrell, PhD

THIS EDITION
Editorial Management by Oriel Square
Produced for DK by WonderLab Group LLC
Jennifer Emmett, Erica Green, Kate Hale, *Founders*

Editors Grace Hill Smith, Libby Romero, Michaela Weglinski;
Photography Editors Kelley Miller, Annette Kiesow, Nicole DiMella;
Managing Editor Rachel Houghton; **Designers** Project Design Company; **Researcher** Michelle Harris;
Copy Editor Lori Merritt; **Indexer** Connie Binder; **Proofreader** Larry Shea;
Reading Specialist Dr. Jennifer Albro; **Curriculum Specialist** Elaine Larson

Published in the United States by DK Publishing
1745 Broadway, 20th Floor, New York, NY 10019

Copyright © 2023 Dorling Kindersley Limited
DK, a Division of Penguin Random House LLC
23 24 25 26 27 10 9 8 7 6 5 4 3 2 1
001–333457–Apr/2023

All rights reserved.
Without limiting the rights under the copyright reserved
above, no part of this publication may be reproduced, stored
in or introduced into a retrieval system, or transmitted, in any
form, or by any means (electronic, mechanical, photocopying,
recording, or otherwise), without the prior written permission
of the copyright owner.
Published in Great Britain by Dorling Kindersley Limited

A catalog record for this book
is available from the Library of Congress.
HC ISBN: 978-0-7440-6799-6
PB ISBN: 978-0-7440-6800-9

DK books are available at special discounts when purchased
in bulk for sales promotions, premiums, fundraising, or
educational use. For details, contact: DK Publishing Special Markets,
1745 Broadway, 20th Floor, New York, NY 10019
SpecialSales@dk.com

Printed and bound in China

The publisher would like to thank the following for their kind permission to reproduce their images:
a=above; c=center; b=below; l=left; r=right; t=top; b/g=background
Dorling Kindersley: Tina Gong 10c; **Dreamstime.com:** Luca Gialdini 20, Ingrid Prats / Titania1980 3;
Getty Images / iStock: strmko 4-5; **Shutterstock.com:** Sergius Bleicher 24-25, Rich Carey 10-11, Diman_Diver 21,
Rostislav Stefanek 26-27, Stock for you 19cra
Cover images: *Front:* **Dreamstime.com:** John Anderson b, Artisticco Llc; *Back:* **Dreamstime.com:** Andrii Symonenko bl
All other images © Dorling Kindersley

For the curious
www.dk.com

Level 1

Explore the Coral Reef

Deborah Lock

Contents

- **6** Coral
- **8** Sea Turtles
- **10** Seahorses
- **13** Sea Stars
- **14** Jellyfish
- **16** Sharksx
- **18** Octopuses

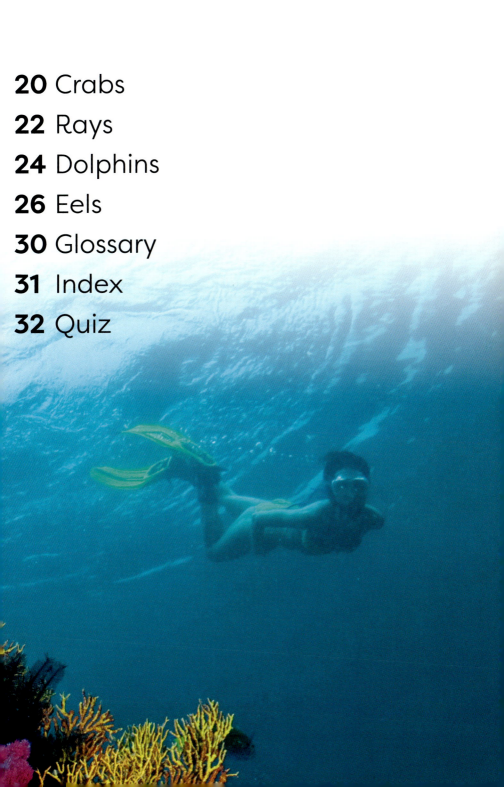

20 Crabs
22 Rays
24 Dolphins
26 Eels
30 Glossary
31 Index
32 Quiz

Coral

Here is a coral reef.

What animals do you see?

coral

fish

Sea Turtles

The sea turtles play in the ocean.

shell

Seahorses

The seahorses sway to and fro.

tail

Sea Stars

Sea stars crawl on the ocean floor.

13

Jellyfish

Jellyfish float up and down in the ocean.

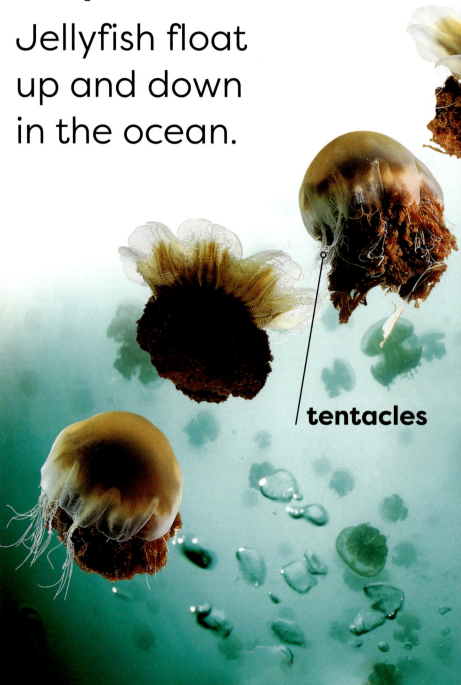

tentacles

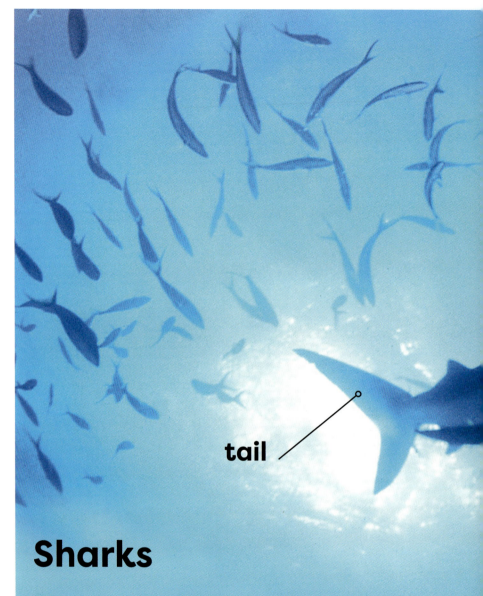

tail

Sharks

Here comes a shark.
It looks for food.

Octopuses

An octopus shoots off to hide.

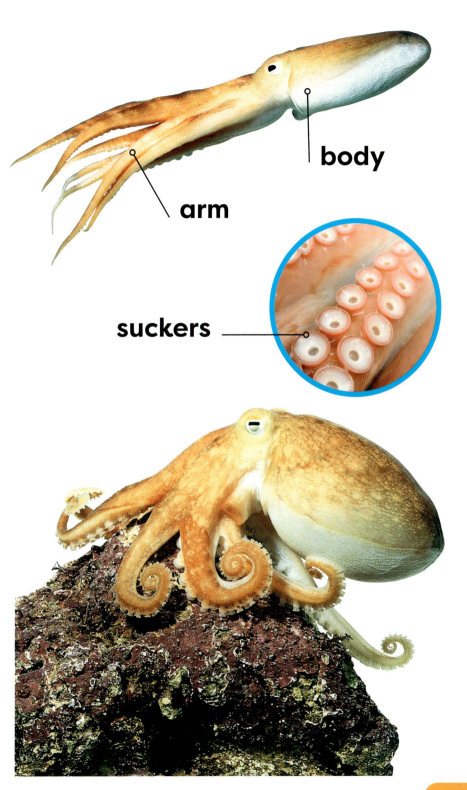

body

arm

suckers

19

Crabs

Crabs hide in the coral and inside big shells.

Rays

A ray hides on the ocean floor.

tail

hiding

Dolphins

A dolphin swims away. It moves its tail up and down.

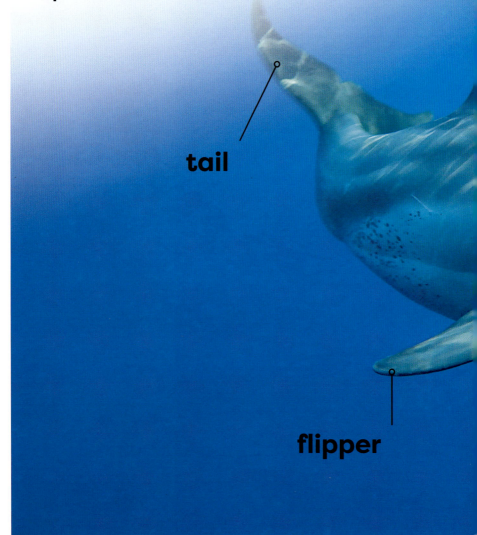

tail

flipper

Eels

An eel looks out for the shark.

eye

fin

tail

The shark swims away.

Glossary

eel
a snake-like fish

octopus
a sea animal with eight long arms

ray
a flat fish with large wing-like fins

sea star
a sea animal with five arms shaped like a star

sea turtle
a marine reptile with a domed shell

Index

claw 21
coral 6, 7, 20
crabs 20
dolphins 24
eels 26
fin 11, 17, 23, 27
fish 7
flipper 9, 24
gills 29
jellyfish 14
octopuses 18

rays 22
sea stars 13
sea turtles 8
seahorses 10
sharks 16, 28
shell 8, 20, 21
snout 11
tail 10, 16, 22, 24, 27
tentacles 14
turtles 8

Quiz

Answer the questions to see what you have learned. Check your answers with an adult.

Which sea animal am I?

1. I have flippers and a hard shell.

2. I have a bell and tentacles.

3. I have long arms covered in suckers.

4. I hide in coral and inside big shells.

5. I am a fish with a long tail and small fins.

1. A sea turtle 2. A jellyfish 3. An octopus
4. A crab 5. An eel